T0198637

Healing
Humanity *From*
Behind the
Shears

Jennifer Zerba

BALBOA.
PRESS

A DIVISION OF HAY HOUSE

Balboa Press books may be ordered through booksellers or by contacting:

Balboa Press
A Division of Hay House
1663 Liberty Drive
Bloomington, IN 47403
www.balboapress.com
1 (877) 407-4847

Because of the dynamic nature of the Internet, any web addresses or
links contained in this book may have changed since publication and
may no longer be valid. The views expressed in this work are solely those
of the author and do not necessarily reflect the views of the publisher,
and the publisher hereby disclaims any responsibility for them.

The author of this book does not dispense medical advice or prescribe
the use of any technique as a form of treatment for physical, emotional,
or medical problems without the advice of a physician, either directly
or indirectly. The intent of the author is only to offer information
of a general nature to help you in your quest for emotional and
spiritual well-being. In the event you use any of the information in
this book for yourself, which is your constitutional right, the author
and the publisher assume no responsibility for your actions.

Any people depicted in stock imagery provided by Thinkstock are
models, and such images are being used for illustrative purposes only.
Certain stock imagery © Thinkstock.

Print information available on the last page.

ISBN: 978-1-5043-3372-6 (sc)
ISBN: 978-1-5043-3373-3 (hc)
ISBN: 978-1-5043-3374-0 (e)

Library of Congress Control Number: 2015909025

Balboa Press rev. date: 07/23/2015

CONTENTS

ABOUT JENNIFER ZERBA

Jennifer has been cutting hair since the age of 5 when her sister needed a bang trim for school pictures. After years of consulting with her own beautician, Stell, on the skills of a good hair dresser, she learned finally at the age of 10 listening was the only skill needed.

Being a licensed Cosmetologist for over 24 years has taught Jennifer that we are always at the right place at the right time and there are No coincidences. She has worked for Corporate Salons, Rented a booth and worked commission in Wyoming and Missouri.

10 years ago during the attainment of her Associates in Business Administration the desire to inspire and motivate an audience drew Jennifer to Toastmasters. She has spoken and presented in front of a few to hundreds of people helping to give them the tools to achieve their hopes and dreams.

Jennifer has a deep commitment to the betterment of humanity and our world. By working with people to help them understand that they are of value, she is convinced that the future will be so bright we will need shades.

ACKNOWLEDGMENTS

Thank you to my children, husband, and family who have shown me how to continue to grow and be a better person.

To those who unconditionally saw in me more than I could see in myself, I am forever grateful to have found you!

FOREWORD

Jennifer is coming out from behind "the shears".

I had thought the gals and guys cutting, dyeing hair, polishing nails were just doing that. Wrong!!! So much is going on with our intimate connection. Jennifer is in touch with this healing energy. She is going to spread the word of what <u>really</u> goes on "Behind the Shears".

She is a joy and a blessing for our planet. You go Girl!!!

~Bill Hayes, D.C., Acupuncturist

INTRODUCTION

Do you wonder if what you are doing is what you are supposed to be doing? Do you wonder if you are in the right place and time? Do you ask how is it I am here doing what it is I am doing? These are some of life's big questions.

It is so easy to look back and follow the events that led up to now. Not so easy to look ahead and know where you will end up. You can look back and understand exactly why situations turned out the way they did. For me, reflection is something I find myself lost in frequently. Who am I, why am I here and most importantly, am I doing what I am supposed to be doing to achieve my mission and my purpose.

Within the mist of my own reflection I realized that I am doing exactly what I am supposed to be doing and that I have always done exactly what I am supposed to be doing. It does not matter what profession or career I have had. There has always been one core element. That element is working with people to help them understand that they are of value. While this may sound like an easy concept, the reality is in our world humans overwhelmingly feel separate, alone and worthless. A concept led by materialism, success, competition, suffering, suppression and a thirst for superiority.

One can simply observe their surroundings for validation. The stench of social decay is overwhelming. The lack of awareness for collective compassion is rampant. There is fictional focus on everything that creates and confirms fear.

We find ourselves nourishing a mask many spiritualists call the ego. This fear is fed by our emotional, physical and spiritual environment. Fear then dictates our life and poisons our minds convincing us that we are isolated from everyone else. Dr. Wayne Dyer says the ego is Edging God Out. I have always resonated with this description. God is love. Ego is not love.

Fear makes us believe just as powerfully as love makes us believe. It is this belief that gives us our definition of value. A closer examination of value is a monetary price we put on possessions. A belief in what something is worth not just to us but also to someone else. The irony is that belief and value should not be connected but they have been intrinsically linked in the minds of humans.

Do you believe you are of value? Do you believe you are of value in your career? Do you believe you are of value in relationships? Do you believe you are of value in your family? Do you believe you are of value in your community, country or world? More importantly, do you believe those around you are of value?

It is my intent to help you, the forgotten unconditional givers of beauty, realize that not only are you of value but indispensable healers for humanity and our world.

Love, *Jen* ~

PART I

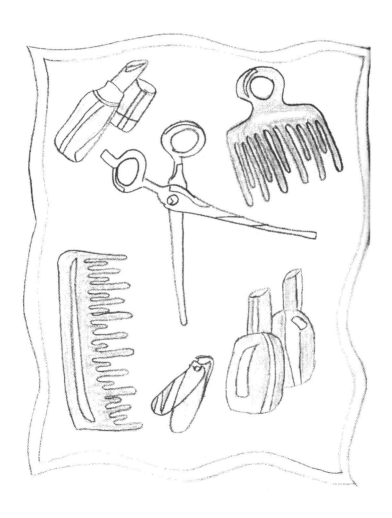

1

To Touch and To Trust

Our journey begins early on a Tuesday morning around 7:30am. A few people are gathering to discuss what happened over the weekend with a cup of coffee, complimenting each other on pretty much anything, and waiting for their clients to arrive. Welcome to the place where magic, aesthetics, prayer and healing meld...The Salon!

No, this is not your typical place of work. This is a place where the art of touch heals people from the moment they book an appointment until the instant they see and feel the finished masterpiece.

Touch is a significant part of what we do as cosmetologists.

When I first started cosmetology school, I remember talking to my step grandmother, Lennie, who owned Town and Country Beauty Salon. She had enduring advice for me. She told me to always remember we are ONE of three professions licensed to touch people. She mentioned that those in the medical field and massage therapists are the only other ones. That is pretty incredible considering all of the different professions and careers available! Taking that a step further, we are the only licensed professionals who see the beauty within and manifest that vision into a work of art that helps people love themselves. They see the beauty we see in them.

From the time our client walks in we begin a choreographed dance of listening, communicating and executing an exquisite living sculpture all while touching them with our hands, mind and heart. It is our gift of knowledge and abilities that transform people to look and feel their best.

Sometimes this transformation is more challenging than others, especially when the person is doing their hair color and/or perms at home. However; we have all been there, either in the stylist chair or styling someone who feels absolutely, positively horrible. We hear the words yucky, gross, miserable, disgusting, frumpy and homely describing how they are feeling and looking about themselves. Sadly we have used those same descriptions about ourselves. Two of my favorite descriptions are "I want something new" or "do what you want". These can be a blessing or a curse.

We hope and pray that somewhere in the back room is a magic potion that will make everything fabulous. We put on an apron and gloves. We mix up the necessary ingredients and in some extreme cases pray to anyone who is listening. It does not matter if the person is a child, teenager, man or woman, they are trusting us to make the impossible possible. I believe that is where the saying "I am a beautician, not a magician" came from! These people are trusting us to make pictures and dreams come to life.

The culmination of touch and trust is that transcendental moment when you have exceeded their expectations and your own. They LOVE their hair and themselves more than they have in a long time or their entire life and they cry and you cry. We have all been there. It is truly the most addictive and amazing feeling in the world, getting it right!

I am convinced that touch and trust go hand in hand more in this industry than in any other because we are licensed to touch people; therefore, our clients trust us. This trust surpasses our client's hair and penetrates their lives. It has been said that more people are loyal and trusting of their hairdresser than their psychiatrists and even spouses when it comes to advice.

This advice has included simple topics such as wardrobe, to marriage counseling, dating advice, child rearing, health, wellness and more serious subjects such as addiction and abuse. In fact some salons have protocol to help battered women find a shelter.

We always have our clients' back and each others'. There is not another profession quite like Cosmetology where not only do our clients support us, but so do our fellow stylists. This is where being nice matters and being kind is rewarded.

Note to Self

1. I Am Healing

2. I Am Trusting

3. I Am Love

NOTES

NOTES

2

Mission Possible

During the chaos of the day, do you ever wonder why you chose to be a cosmetologist? Do you believe that you have a mission and purpose? What is your mission and purpose as a cosmetologist? More importantly, what is your mission and purpose as a human being?

Going to cosmetology school for me was a goal I had wanted to achieve since 10 years old. I didn't know why other than beauticians were amazing. They could see a picture someone picked out and then cut, style, perm or color it on that person and make that person look like the picture. I thought they were really magicians.

During school I found natural talents for listening to people describe what they wanted and seeing what they were talking about in my mind. Sometimes during the consultation when my vision and what they were saying conflicted, I found myself asking more questions until the picture in my head and what they were talking about matched. As my abilities grew, so did my confidence. I challenged my instructors to know more and do more. I could see myself being successful in this industry.

Skills were something throughout my career that continued to grow. Working for corporate owned salons enabled me to have one on one training in aspects of technique and product knowledge. Renting my own station and working for commission enabled me to attend hair shows and once again learning more technique and product knowledge.

At work my tool box of skills was growing and improving. However; I found myself frequently asking life's big questions. It was then that my desire to study spirituality began to grow. I had discrepancies and questions that my childhood religious upbringing and mainstream fundamental traditions could not answer. Over the next 20 years I began seeking and studying inspirational, motivational, and spiritual people, speakers and authors.

My most significant spiritual influence is my friends Frank and Karen who taught me "the secret" 20 years ago. Be careful what you think. While the book of the same name has become a household name today, back then it was a new concept to me.

One of my favorite motivational people is Tony Robbins. He exemplifies the power of passion through his vivacious energy. He teaches people how to empower themselves and never settle.

Inspirational people I have learned from include famous people like Oprah, Gandhi, and Deepak

Chopra to my own hairdresser and massage therapist. It is easy to find inspiration when you choose to look for it, such as a flower, a puppy, and the Walmart checkout clerk.

Just as we all are trained to limit ourselves to a job description, I was trained to define myself as a beauty operator. During the last 14 years; however, I yearned to hear, see, and learn more about a higher purpose for what it is I was doing as a cosmetologist.

My spiritual study taught me an awareness that what I do is a divine mission that serves a greater purpose on a humanitarian level. It is subtle and incredibly powerful. It is the transformation of a lost and desperate soul trying to find itself. It is a transformation of a sick person needing to be healed.

As Cosmetologists, our purpose instead of just service needs to be of healing through art on an emotional, physical and mental level. This begins the moment they book their appointment and the interaction of emotions between us and them. When we think about them our thoughts can either begin healing them or creating fear. When our clients walk into the salon our thoughts have already laid the ground work for what is about to transpire in our chair. Will they have hope we can help OR will they be scared?

Take for example the desperate client who sits in our chair. When we consult with them and hear what is going on with their hair they are sad and depressed. The desperation can vary from simply needing a trim, to a new client who has had several horrible experiences that have scarred them for life. Either way it is up to us to know our talent creates art that will heal them.

How do you use your talent to heal your clients? How do you heal those around you? Do you show compassion? Do you show understanding? Do you simply listen with your heart? When your client sits in your chair do you touch them on the shoulder? They know you care. Do you look them directly in the eye (not in the mirror) and actively listen? They know you understand. Do you take the extra time at the shampoo bowl helping them relax? They know you unwind them. Do you make them the center of your attention? They know you are concerned about them. Do you finish your masterpiece with a style that will help them feel better about themselves? They feel good. Do you protect your work, their hair and scalp with appliance and product suggestions? They know you are concerned about them. Do you schedule their next appointment or appointments? They know you are in this together.

If you have trouble with being confident in your skill, I encourage you to continue your education anyway you can. Watch technical videos to enhance your toolbox of skills. Go to hair shows to learn the newest and most current trends. Take a communication class or join a local Toastmasters Club to improve your leadership and communication skills!

When we INTEND healing, our abilities are amplified! We have the skill to heal everyone we lay our hands on. The healing starts with their heads, goes beyond their minds and flows into their hearts. As cosmetologists we are healers. Our mission and purpose is clear: make our world a beautiful place!

NOTES

NOTES

3

Meant To Be

Another day has ended and several clients have walked into the salon and many of them have sat in our chair. Have you ever considered the bigger picture? The bigger picture where everyone and everything we have come into contact with was MEANT to be? What if there are no coincidences? What if there is karma or even group karma?

This may be a strange concept for some of us. The notion that we were supposed to have the cranky and difficult client or the idea that the argument we had with a fellow stylist was orchestrated on a higher level. What about a fellow stylist's client? Were we supposed to meet them too? Of course we are! In the book "Celestine Prophecy" by James Redfield he talks about the fact there are no coincidences. Everything happens for a reason. Here's a kicker: you and the cranky client and your fellow stylist agreed and were joined together to help each other's mission and purpose.

We are all familiar with this when reflecting back upon situations that have happened to us. If we l our spouse or significant other. If we hadn't gone shopping at that exact moment, we wouldn't have met a high school friend who invited us to that amazing party where we met the love of our life. It is humbling and incredible to think how everything had to happen in order for that simple meeting to take place, or is it?

What if it is simply how things work? What if the symphony of life is independently played out by each of us to create a beautiful piece of music? We asked for someone special to spend our life with. We saw the opportunity and we moved on it maybe because we saw that the stars were lined up.

Sometimes these events come into our lives to give us a message. This message comes from adversity with others such as the cranky and difficult client for they are our greatest teachers that help us grow in kindness, patience and compassion. These scenarios benefit us in the most miraculous ways by forcing us to grow. They are simply a reflection of what we don't like in and about ourselves. The reflection has been magnified by the perfect teacher(s) of our choosing.

Be mindful of these openings, for they can benefit or hinder your growth not only personally but also professionally. Take for example once the client leaves, are you angry and hateful or are you loving and grateful? Each one of these paths can lead you down a different direction. Each direction is amplified with that fear or that love you thought, spoke or acted on.

Karma, the law of cause and effect, is not revered by many in the American culture. The thought that what you send out with your thoughts, words and actions you get back is really nothing new. For example, *The Secret* by Rhonda Byrne was a huge success selling millions of copies worldwide teaching readers the concept that thoughts become things. Science has proven, philosophy has postulated and religion has preached this fundamental universal law that is rarely observed.

Living Karma in the salon creates an atmosphere and awareness that allows and encourages us all to honor, to love and to respect each other. Now take a moment to visualize a working environment where living Karma is practiced. All people are loved. All people are valued. All people are appreciated. How does this happen? How can it happen when one person ruins it for everyone? More importantly, how can one person change the negative culture in a salon? Be conscious of you! What are you thinking? What are you saying? What are you doing? If you follow the path of love then love will come to you in its entire glorious splendor of abundance, joy, passion and inspiration.

When working in a hostile environment NO ONE benefits. The continuation of back stabbing, hateful drama perpetuates a cesspool of negativity that poisons our body, mind and spirit. Just as the "Law of Attraction" works to bring goodness and wellness to our lives when we think, speak and act in goodness and wellness, and so it does to bring anger, frustration and chaos when we think in these ways too.

Have you ever worked in a salon where negativity was the name of the game? How did this atmosphere make you feel? Did you dread going to work? Did you experience sickness? The virus of gossiping is very contagious. Do you or others gossip about clients, people in the community, or maybe other stylists? What is your role in this engagement? Are you part of the problem or part of the solution?

We are all living this experience together. It is up to us to grow and to help each other grow. Be nice because it matters! The coincidences we perceive are really synchronicities perfectly meant to be.

NOTES

NOTES

4

Passing on the Love

So you have gotten it right. That moment you know you exceeded your client's expectations. They love their hair and they feel amazing. Now what? Has any of your creativity or their experience made a lasting impression? Is your intention for that lasting impression just to keep your client? I know this is a shallow question, but is it your sole intention of building clientele and using all of your energy and work only for the money, and the perpetuation of money?

In the business model, the game is to make money and lots of it. Success and value are measured in dollar amounts. Classes, seminars, workshops and degrees teach individuals how to make more money. On the surface it seems money makes the world go around. Money, however; is not the "be all end all". And despite what some say, the "All Mighty Dollar" is not God. Yes it seems money creates everything both good and bad, but I challenge you to see this as a deterrent for keeping people suppressed and reluctantly accepting of suffering. No one dies wishing they had made more money. The world today is a reflection of the undervalued, unsuccessful, and lost human beings we believe ourselves to be by the trillions of dollars spent on anti depressants, anti anxiety medications, self help books, self help seminars and workshops.

What does this have to do with me? I am only a cosmetologist. All I do is cut, color, and perm hair. Our role as cosmetologists and healers begs for a different intention, and a different direction. When all of the energy and work we give our clients has the intention of love then everything changes. This is when the healing goes beyond the client. When they leave the salon feeling amazing and pass the feeling along.

Now I know what you are thinking...pass along?? We all know that when you feel good, you feel like you can accomplish anything. More importantly you feel good about yourself. This feeling creates a domino effect into every part of your being making it easier to see good, hear good, and feel good. Ok, so here is the super cool kicker: everything you come into contact with is affected by this feeling. When I say everything, I mean everything! The pen you write with, the car you drive, the tree you see, the dog you pet, the checker at the general store. Everything is affected!

Why should this matter? Because YOU have the power to give love or fear to your client with your presence and service. It is up to you to know the difference and understand your impact! Change your intention so all that is passed along makes a positive impact on the world around us.

NOTES

NOTES

PART II

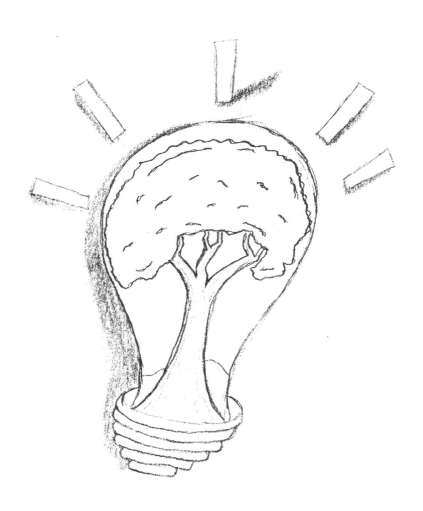

5

Power of Touch

It is said that touch is linked to feelings of compassion and reward. Touch allows cooperative relationships and signals safety and trust; hence, our license to touch is much more powerful than ever imagined. Our touch can signal the release of oxytocin the "love hormone". If this is true, then what about the economic implications of touch? Is it possible touch promotes trust and generosity? According to The Greater Good website the answer is yes! As Cosmetologists, we know this for a fact. Touch does promote trust.

Dr. Bruce Lipton is a former medical school professor and research scientist. In his book "The

Biology of Belief" he along with fellow leading edge colleagues have researched and examined how cells receive and process information. What is amazing and incredible are the implications in our understanding of the universe, of evolution, of our earth and of life. This research showed that our genes and DNA DO NOT control our biology. Instead, signals emanating from our thought forms control the cell from the outside. Outside includes our environment! Our environment isn't the single factor in the type of change that can unfold; it is our perception of the environment. If our environment is healthy and loving we can change the genetics in our body and influence others. Our salon environment then is critically important not only for us, but for everyone who enters it.

In Chapter 3 I talked about negativity in the salon and how it affects everyone. I also talked about your perception of the salon. The salon IS our environment. If we don't take an active part in monitoring and improving the environment, then who will?

Dr. Deepak Chopra is what I would consider a spiritual physician. In his book "Ageless Body, Timeless Mind" he discusses the placebo effect. In medical research, participants are given active pills developed to help their ailments. Placebos, or sugar pills, are also given. The effect of both is then measured. Interestingly enough, brain scans show that a placebo, when effective, changes the brain in the same way as do active pills, and these changes can be found in all parts of the body including the spinal cord and not just the brain. The implications are strong for chronic pain over an extended period, too. Studies in arthritis patients have shown that the placebo effect can last over two years. In sum, belief and intention is more powerful and more long-lasting than is generally realized, even among physicians.

So why does this matter? A placebo is believed to be the "real thing". Your perception makes them work. If what you perceive matters and you are touching someone, wouldn't it make sense that you need to be aware and conscious of what you are thinking, saying and doing? It is so incredible to think that your intention can be measured not only in a laboratory but also in the body and mind of your client, your co-workers and their clients.

Being aware is being in the present or the NOW. Touch has an incredible way of getting us on the fast track to the now. When we love and care for our clients in the now it changes how they feel and changes their body. Stress is an insurmountable delusion in our society today. Try as we may and try as we might with yoga, meditation, pills, drugs and therapy to deal with stress, it is only until our perception or BELIEF changes that stress will be alleviated. Stress involves the release of power chemicals that the body must cut off before it does damage to itself. This is really powerful since we know how relaxing touch can be and therefore healing.

Cosmetologists can use touch therapy to help their clients. While there are numerous certifications for touch therapy, simply our awareness to love our clients during their interaction with us will promote healing.

~ Jen's Happy Healing Hair Protocol~

For first time clients, I smile and shake their hand using both of my hands holding theirs in mine while telling them my name. This reassures them that they are in good hands. When they sit in my chair, I put my hand on their shoulder during an extensive consultation with what they have in mind and to make sure we have the same vision.

For regular clients, when they sit in my chair I still put my hand on their shoulder during the consultation.

Shampooing is the first moment I get to really engage the energy and touch with them. I use techniques such as Reconnection and Circuit Energy while having them breathe using deep belly breaths. This is nasal breathing starting with the inhale belly out for a count of four, hold breathe for a count of four, exhale belly in through for a count of four, hold breathe for a count of four. This is all done while I am giving a massaging shampoo and condition for 10 minutes. The purpose of this is more than a clean scalp and hair, but to relax and increase their oxygen intake while enjoying their salon experience.

Research has shown that breathing through the nose is incredibly beneficial for us. Why? Nasal breathing pushes oxygen into our lower lungs unlike mouth breathing; therefore, it eliminates the CO_2 waste efficiently. Have you ever run out of breath? Maybe you were coughing like a chain smoker. Thank your lower lungs! They were working really hard to get that junk out!! Here is something crazy; when nasal breathing is practiced regularly it is actually calming...even during a marathon.

In her book "Jump Start Your Metabolism," Pam Grout talks about geometric breathing. In fact, square breathing using the count of four also increases the level of oxygen in the lungs and therefore the bloodstream.

During the service, conversation and communication continue. The interest and well being of the client is always observed such as offering a magazine, coffee, water and asking if the client is comfortable. For Extra kudos, I would also recommend offering others in the salon coffee or water if you are able. This will help your character sparkle and shine towards fellow stylists and clients. It is also your way of spreading the love around!

At the end of the service communication of the next appointment and handing TWO business cards out is my policy. One card is for them to keep with their next appointment on it and one to give to a friend when they ask "Where did you get that amazing hair?" Give them a final hand shake with both hands and a smile.

I know most stylists have "Their" way of interacting and communicating with clients and other stylists. This may be different and helps to instill in you to work together with an awareness of your mission and purpose of healing and that is to love through your touch.

Note to Self

1. I Am Love

2. I Am Kindness

3. I Am Forgiving

NOTES

NOTES

6

Power of Water

Do you work with water? Do you work in water? What percentage of your body is water? Silly questions, I know! All stylists work with water and our percentage of water in our body and on earth is amazingly 70 – 75 %. But what does that have to do with healing and energy?

The word energy is tossed around today to explain everything from wavelengths to frequency, to vibration, to consciousness. What does energy mean to you? And don't limit it to turning on the light or what your two year old has that you wish could be bottled up. How does energy affect you in the salon or with your client? Is there energy in service? Is there energy in love?

The simple answer is yes. Energy can be felt and seen. An internationally renowned Japanese researcher, Dr. Masaru Emoto, in his book "Hidden Messages in Water" and "Love Thyself" show conclusively our connection to water by our individual and collective consciousness. By taking pictures of water crystals he discovered something very interesting. When the water was focused with prayers, thoughts, pictures or music of love and kindness, the result was a beautifully formed crystalline structure. To the contrary, when the water was focused with the playing of heavy metal music, writing words on the bottle like "I hate you", "You disgust me" it resulted in fragmented and malformed crystals that look sick and deformed. Literally it looks like a cesspool of toxic negativity!

If that is the case then as stylists, we have the privilege and obligation to help our clients and ourselves to have love in our awareness and project the love. Dr. Emoto's research showed that the vibration of good words has a positive effect even in our world, whereas the vibration from negative words has the incredible power to destroy. When you think, speak and act in love then you will watch in bliss as your skills improve, your results progress and your income escalates.

Note to Self

1. I Am Graceful

2. I Am Elegant

3. I Am Love

NOTES

NOTES

7

Power of Color

Remember beauty school theory on color? We were taught the primary colors of red, yellow and blue. That they make up ALL colors and that in theory when all are mixed together they create black. We worked the color wheel and have helped numerous clients out of a bad spot when they turned their hair orange or green. That same fabulous color wheel helped US out when we lifted the hair to a beautiful papaya and then needed to tone. All of this is true and useful. But where does color come from? Why do we see papaya in the hair or too much ash? How is color energy? How can both visible and non-visible color heal?

It wasn't until Newton that we understood the role light has in color sensation. Color is derived from a spectrum of light interacting with our eyes and their light receptors. The color of an object such as hair depends on two factors. The first factor is the physics of the object in its environment for example the client who always sees their hair ash in their bathroom because most of the colors in the bathroom are green. The second factor is perception due to an individual's eye and how their brain communicates for example when you and your client don't see the too gold tones in her hair.

Visible color has been regarded as having only aesthetic qualities, pleasing to matters of taste, making a certain call upon the emotions; there are bright colors and subdued colors, enlightening and depressing, pleasant and unpleasant, all according to the taste of the observer, but there is a definite therapeutic value as well. This therapeutic matter called Chromotherapy is of less common knowledge and the basis of color treatment where one vibrating body will produce similar vibrations in another body that is sufficiently in tune with it.

Using color to heal or compliment a person's state of mind is just the beginning. People are drawn to colors for their hair and attire for certain reasons. The sayings "blondes have more fun" or "fiery red head" or "brainy brunette" have some truth to it. Changing ones hair color affects ones attitude which can lead to changes in life. If you are feeling sad or blue wear something that will brighten and lift your spirits such as orange. Could it be that a little fire is needed to lift a person out of the blues? Just as with color corrections, you can utilize your skills and apply them to the wardrobe or hair. An entire book could be written on stylists using color correction to heal their clients through hair and apparel.

Don't be afraid to step outside of the "norm". There are only two places you will ever see audiences of people wearing black. They are either at a funeral OR at a hair show. Someone somewhere thought cosmetologists need to wear black to look professional. Toss that idea into the circular file and stop the insanity! No one wants to have a funeral director make them feel better, or look beautiful...unless they are dead. We are NOT dead, find your color palette. Take a class; go to a workshop or seminar. Do whatever it takes and begin to be the source for your client's inspiration of fashion. People who wear or are attracted to black clothes are looking to feel grounded. Usually this is because their lives are in chaos or scattered or they were told it was professional. Stacy London and Clinton Kelly from "What Not To Wear" would have a field day at a hair show!

All color has a related wavelength, frequency, vibration and sound for which it can be measured. Red, for example, will have a slower and longer wavelength, frequency and vibration with a lower tone than purple which will have a faster and shorter wavelength, frequency and vibration with a higher tone.

The non-visible spectrum functions the same way. Many are unaware that this particular spectrum of light exists around EVERYTHING! Those who are aware of it may use the term aura.

According to Google the term Aura means:

1. "The distinctive atmosphere or quality that seems to surround and be generated by a person, place or thing."

2. "a supposed emanation surrounding the body of a living creature, viewed by mystics, spiritualists, and some practitioners of complementary medicine as the essence of the individual, and allegedly discernible by people with special sensibilities.

3. "any invisible emanation, especially a scent or odor".

Today the idea of one seeing an aura is mostly scoffed at by the scientific community, but it has not always been that way. In fact some of the most famous paintings by Michelangelo and Leonardo Da Vinci depict light around the heads of Jesus, Mary and Saints. Similar to what a halo would look like. Ancient Egyptian art depicts auras. Chinese culture calls it Chi. Sanskrit refers to it as Prana.

Today certain people are born seeing auras while others can learn to see them. For those who are short of patience to learn to see auras, there is Kirlian photography. This special photography will show not only your aura and the incredibly beautiful colors it holds, but also that of anything put on sheet photographic film. The result in every instance is light emanating from the object whether it is white light or separated into its component colors.

People who see auras describe the same thing. Primarily light has been separated into its component colors by various factors. These factors can range from health, emotion, intention, to thoughts and communication. Individuals who are in tune with this sight are known to see where the body is sick, if the person is sad, and even if the person is telling the truth.

It was thought that the aura surrounded and stayed with the individual or object. This is not the case. Those who have this sight report seeing aura's or energy fields connect and affect others energy fields; therefore, visually validating unified field of consciousness. We are all connected. "We", meaning the cell phone, the shampoo bowl to the gossiping next door neighbor.

To take this a step further, these people can also see what emotion, intention, and thought is being sent taking communication to a whole new level. Gary Zukav in *Seat of the Soul* talks about intention with great passion and detail. Imagine being able to see your intention! Imagine seeing the intention of those around you? Imagine seeing a pair of shoes surrounded by a pink light and that pink light is being directed to you!

Jennifer Zerba

Some may view this sight as a gift. Others may view this as a curse. Don't make the mistake of trying to cover your intention with bologna. People may not always be able to see your intention but they sure do feel it. Have you ever said, "I just felt they were in it for the money"? Most likely they were. As a healer in the salon, intention is the back bone of every service you give.

NOTES

NOTES

PART III

"Gratitude, Kindness, Positivity"

8

Daily Method of Operation

Every person has a crazy busy life and it can be so demanding that taking time out for one's self seems almost impossible. Making simple life changes a habit can be challenging, and at times it can seem overwhelming. But it does not have to be with K.I.S.S., Keep It Seriously Simple. I know there is so much information to absorb, digest and bring into daily life. That you may be asking yourself: "Where do I start?" You start with a D.M.O. Daily Method of Operation filled with gratitude, kindness and positivity.

Sounds simple doesn't it? Start your day even before getting out of bed thinking about everything you are grateful for. It may be difficult in the beginning for some, but K.I.S.S. Are you grateful to wake up? Are you grateful to open your eyes? Are you grateful for the sheets on your bed? Are you grateful for the blanket? Now look around and enjoy seeing. Now feel your sheets and enjoy feeling them. Now feel the warmth of your spot in the bed.

With gratitude in heart think of how amazing it is you are alive. How incredible it is you have the gift of sight and how it enables you to create this art we call Cosmetology. How humbling it is you have sheets when your client may not. How fortunate you have a blanket when your neighbor may not.

Now with gratitude and kindness in your heart, smile. Be happy. Be positive and tell yourself today is a fantastic day. Tell yourself today is filled with laughter, joy, love. Whatever you want to happen that day know, "As I proclaim it, so it shall be!"

People don't spend enough time with this practice of gratitude, kindness and positivity. It will set up your day like nothing you have ever done! Your heart and body will sing, vibrating at an angelic level.

Continue with a quick 5 minute stretching and deep breathing practice. Dr. John Douillard's *3 Season Diet* has an amazing fat burning sequence designed to balance all three Ayurvedic doshas of Vatta, Pitta, and Kapha which I have thoroughly enjoyed! These 5 minutes of stretching with deep nasal breathing wakes up your internal organs for the day and gets them burning fat. Follow with his Twelve Minute Workout – Sprint Recovery Training! Yes I said 12 minutes!!! Start with a 2 minute warm up or use the 5 minute fat burning stretch using nasal breathing. Then sprint with a cardio quick pace workout such as jumping jacks for one minute using nasal breathing. Then recover with nasal breathing for 90 seconds. Do this for three intervals. Cool down for 2 minutes or do the 5 minute fat burning stretch. You can find out more in his web article *Be Fit, Thin & Calm in 12 Minutes a Day*. This is also a wonderful time for 20 minutes of meditation. I enjoy meditating to Dr. Dyer's CD *I Am Wishes Fulfilled Meditation*.

Gratitude, Kindness and Positivity will work synergistically together. The more you think, say and act with these, the more you will manifest. *Law of Attraction* by Abraham Hicks and *Wishes Fulfilled* by Dr. Wayne Dyer are two incredible resources for those wishing additional information.

Mindfulness is meditation in motion. Be aware of your surroundings by your five senses for one minute. Smell the shampoo. Feel the shampoo in your hands. Feel your feet securely planted on the floor. Are they balanced? Hear the lather starting quiet and getting louder. Breathe deep belly breaths. Relax.

Use Dr. Douillard's 1 minute meditation. 30 bellow breaths followed by 30 seconds of mindfulness. It truly helps when that one client is grating your last nerve like a block of cheese! You can find more about this in his web article *One Minute Meditation.*

The day is over and it was wonderful! So many fantastic things happened. You helped people feel better about themselves. You got groceries picked up AND you made it to the kid's choir concert on time. The day was truly great. Are you grateful? Write it down! At the end of the day have a gratitude journal by your bed side to review your grateful day. List everything that was amazing, incredible and wonderful. Use the words I Am grateful for...... with each event.

After your gratitude journaling, begin your I Am intentions list to sleep on! Once again use the words I Am...... The Notes To Self at the end of every chapter is a great start. I Am Love. I Am Joy. I Am Prosperous. I Am Healthy. As you sleep you are aligning yourself with these intentions. When you awaken you will feel alive and ready to start the cycle of gratitude, kindness and positivity again.

Do not be afraid to utilize this sequence on everyone and everything. You are now aware that what you think, say and do affects the rock on the street, to the car you drive, to the perm you put on your clients hair. The change is now a habit and it was seriously simple!

Use this daily method of operation and watch your world transform into one that reflects all the love, joy, and kindness the universe has to offer. Be a role model by thinking, speaking and acting as though everything and everyone has value because you know you have value. My family of artisans go forth with this knowing and heal humanity from behind the shears!

Note to Self

1. I Am Grateful that Michelle is cancer free

2. I Am Grateful that mom called today

3. I Am Grateful that Steven has a new job

4. I Am Grateful that I made Mrs. Smith look 20 Years younger

Note to Self

1. I Am Rampage
2. I Am Healing
3. I Am Trusting
4. I Am Love
5. I Am Compassion
6. I Am Therapeudic
7. I Am Abundant
8. I Am Joy
9. I Am Valued
10. I Am Brave
11. I Am Kindness
12. I Am Forgiving

NOTES

NOTES

RECOMMENDED READING

>*Law of Attraction* by Abraham-Hicks

>*Wishes Fulfilled* by Dr. Wayne Dyer

>*Ageless Body, Timeless Mind: The Quantum Alternative to Growing Old* by Dr. Deepak Chopra

>*The Biology of Belief* by Dr. Bruce Lipton

>*The Hidden Messages in Water* by Masuru Emoto

>*The 3-Season Diet* by Dr. John Douillard

>*Jump Start Your Metabolism* by Pam Grout

NOTES

NOTES

Printed in the United States
By Bookmasters